Lois Wilson

LIKE A
MIGHTY
RIVER

*"Let justice flow down like
a river, and righteousness
like a mighty stream."*
Amos 24:5

Jim Taylor photo

WOOD LAKE PRESS
Winfield, B.C.   Toronto, Ont.
1981

ISBN 0-919599-01-X

Published by
Wood Lake Press

Head Office
S-6, C-9, R.R. 1
Winfield, BC
V0H 2C0

Branch Office
21 Tulane Crescent
Don Mills, ON
M3A 2B9

Canada

First Printing 1981
Second Printing 1982
Third Printing 1982

Printed and bound in Canada by
Friesen Printers
a Division of D.W. Friesen & Sons Ltd.
Altona, Manitoba, R0G 0B0
Canada

CONTENTS

FOREWORD

I agreed to write a foreword for Lois Wilson's book "Like A Mighty River" partly because I have known Lois for many years and owe much to her, her parents, brothers and sisters, and her husband. My associations with them are "a part of me", a part for which I am deeply grateful.

I did follow my firm practice that I would not write a foreword without having at least skimmed the draft manuscript. I have done more than skim it. I have read it (in rough draft) carefully, parts of it several times. This has made me deeply thankful that I agreed to write the foreword, but has also made the writing far more difficult. What shall I say? Words fail me. I knew before I started to write I would always need "one more word" to begin to express what I want to express. What I want to say cannot be expressed adequately in words but they are a means of trying to convey thoughts and concerns so I use them for this purpose, admitting my and their inadequacies.

I hope and pray that many people will read Lois's book, so short and yet so vitally important. I hope and pray that it will shock many who read it for we desperately need to be shocked, shocked out of complacency into awareness, out of apathy into action, out of despair into hope, out of superficial faith into struggle, and I believe this book can help this to happen.

Lois, in a very short period, has exposed herself in depth to reality situations in many parts of our one world, situations many ignore and keep away from. She has an incredible ability, for which I am deeply grateful, to express the perceptions gained from such exposure in short, telling statements, composed of simple, direct words that help people to see the key issues at the heart of a particular situation or experience. She has an ability, which few possess, to communicate her keen personal experiences with people who have not had them.

Lois's decision to so express herself to existing world situations directly has not made life easy for her, either as a person or in her role as the first woman Moderator of the United Church of Canada. Reading her book will not make life easy for readers. It will test their faith. It will make it virtually impossible to give an easy reason for the faith that is in them. It will lead them, as she acknowledges her experiences led her, to pray one of the deepest prayers recorded in scripture; "Lord I believe, help thou mine unbelief", the prayer that comes when we really admit our dependence on God.

This leads me to a further comment. Another of Lois's many abilities is to be able to link her experiences in a living way with the Bible. Biblical insights come alive in stark terms in the cruel, hard, demanding realities of our world which are made clear for us to see in her writing. Not only does she make these realities clear for us to see, she also poses the basic question for herself and for her readers, "What am I, what are you, going to do in the face of these realities?" Consciously or unconsciously, because we go on living, each of us makes some response to these realities.

May each of us pray in her words, "Lord, we long to be washed by your living waters, so that 'Justice shall roll on like a river and righteousness like an ever flowing stream'," and pray, also, in the words from an ancient prayer, "Lord, help us both to perceive and know what we ought to do, and also to have grace and power faithfully to fulfill the same. Amen."

The Most Reverend **Edward W. Scott**
Primate, The Anglican Church of Canada,
Moderator, The Central Committee of
The World Council of Churches.

LIVING WATER

**Exploring
a New World**

As a doe longs for running streams
So longs my soul for you, O God.
My soul thirsts for God, the God of life.'

(Psalm 42:1, Jer. Bible)

So often, in shared reflection with my hosts in Asia,
Central and South America,
we spoke of water   clean
                    clear
                        running
                            life-giving
                                abundant

Because so often it was polluted
                            murky
                                stagnant
                                    death-dealing
                                        scarce

This book is for people who need clean water to drink;
for the parched ones who pant after
'living water, welling up into eternal life.'

for the thirsty land

and for all who pray for justice
'that rolls on like a river
and righteousness
like an ever-flowing stream.'

A NEW WORLD

I am flying in one of those 747's … movies …
lots of food and drink.
The crew speak English and French.

'This is how to use your life preserver.'
(It is five hours over the Atlantic, isn't it?)

A change in London … Another 747 …
The crew speak English and Hindi.

Huge snowcapped mountains bursting through clouds.
The Austrian Alps. Think of the skiing!

Five and a half hours later, we put down in Tehran.
A city of four million people, and I'm not even sure
which *country* we're in.

A midnight drive through wide, spacious streets:

flat roofs
mosques decorated with blue mosaic tile
mountains at the end of the street
construction everywhere
beautifully laid out gardens
Christmas cards with Persian motif
soldiers carrying guns.

And we passengers, until now strangers, began to talk.

A Trinidadian doctor, going to India
to the World Mental Health Association.

A Church of England sister,
going to her post in Bangladesh.

A newlywed from Kenya, living in London,
on her way to visit parents in Delhi.

A nine year old Indian boy from Vancouver,
to Delhi to visit his grandmother.

All these strange faces, and different people.
Not one of them like me.

'Yet God has made of one blood
all the nations
to dwell on the face of the earth.'

Acts 17: 26

Must we learn to love them?
Do we even want to know how?

WHAT'S IN A NAME?

For Asians, 'Lois Wilson' is as difficult
as 'So-Chu Kwang' is for me!

In my travels
I met people with interesting names:
        Ildes
         Ithamar
          Zwingli
           Enilson
            Onesimus

And interesting place names:
    Eyebrow, Saskatchewan
     Seldom Come By, Newfoundland
      Rest And Be Thankful, Scotland

In the Bible, names reveal the person's essential nature
    Abram becomes Abraham
        and covenants with God
    Jacob becomes Israel
        and contends for God
    Saul becomes Paul
        and becomes a new creation
    Jesus of Nazareth becomes the Christ
        and the Word becomes flesh.

We thank you God — that you not only set the stars in
their courses, but also call each of us by name,
and out of darkness
into your marvelous light.

CROSSING BOUNDARIES

What am I doing
sitting in the airport in Tehran,
drinking a coke bought for me
by the Indian girl from Nairobi?

She lives in London, but is the first Indian in her block,
so she is still very insecure.

Across the aisle sits a woman swathed in a black 'burka,'
face veiled. She's a Muslim.
Why can't she be 'with it' and contemporary,
like me?

Then there's the Sikh, with red turban
who gets into a verbal battle
with the Hindu father of three,
as to who was first in line for boarding the aircraft.

Tempers are short.

I peer out of the window for my first view of desert

> wave after wave of sand
> barren wastes with one thin track
> stretching beyond the horizon
> not a living thing, plant, animal or person.
> Low but rugged mountains …
> for miles
> and miles
> and miles.

We're over Iran, Afganistan, Pakistan, says the pilot.

continued over

Aramco photo

How did the Wise Men ever get through from the east,
to Bethlehem?
The preacher on Epiphany Sunday in Delhi said,
'Wise men aren't necessarily from the east.
Wise men are those that cross boundaries.'

Maybe *that's* why God saw fit to seat me
beside the Indian girl from Nairobi,
the one who bought me a coke.
And opposite the Muslim.

To see if I could.

Cross boundaries, I mean.

INDIA

People
Piled
on
People

The first person I saw in India was a sweeper.
She was squatting on the airport roadway,
clearing away the leaves.

One night I stayed at the United Theological Seminary,
which has over one hundred students,
including some specializing in the media.
I was awakened by the soft sound of sweeping.

At dawn, women bent double
were clearing the seminary pathways of dust.
The brooms they use are only two feet long,
and held in one hand.

I was going to sweep my own room
but that would deprive a 'sweeper'
of her livelihood:
twenty-five cents a day.

The Bangalore newspapers reported an attempt
to guarantee minimum working conditions for sweepers,
some of whom also have the work
of collecting and disposing of human waste
from public places.

Wasn't Martin Luther King assassinated,
in the United States
for marching in solidarity with garbage workers
on strike for better working conditions?

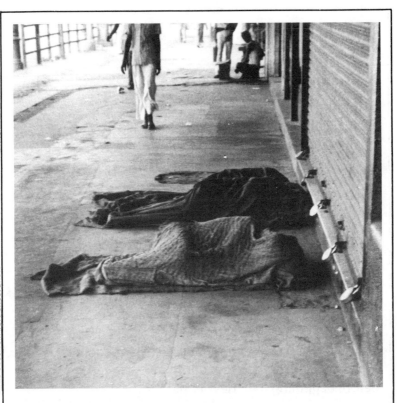

Most sweepers in India are former untouchables,
whom Gandhi renamed 'Harijans,'
meaning 'People of God.'
No wonder they named him 'Mahatma'
which means 'Great Soul.'

> 'The first shall be last
> and the last first'
> in the Kingdom.

Is that true Lord?

Then what happens to middle class people
like me?

BODY LANGUAGE

His hands were cupped,
palms up
arms slightly raised
ready to *receive*.

He was squatting on a mat
imprinted with verses from the Quran
the holy book of Islam …

And rocking back and forth in concentration
passion
supplication.

A lone worshipper in the Jama Masjid Mosque in Delhi
a building as large as St. Peter's in Rome
swarming with men ceremonially washing themselves
in the fountain in the outer courtyard
before beginning their devotions,

surrounded with blind beggars
men urinating at curbside
horns blaring
merchants hawking wares in the outdoor bazaar
families huddled around a small cow dung fire
people sleeping on the steps of the Mosque
tourists climbing the high minaret to take a picture
women with veils covering their faces
the Indian army going through its paces

So many people with hands grasping
taking
selling

And the lone worshipper,
        acting as though everything was quiet
      with immense concentration and humility
          cups his hands,
            palms up
         ready to receive grace.

We Christians need to talk with Muslims.

And learn.

The enormous sandstone and marble mausoleum
is known as 'Humayun's Tomb,'
built in the sixteenth century by his widow.

How can I describe it …
the grand scale?
the acres of garden?

Gov't of India photo

Consider Emperor Akbar's Tomb, in Sikandra.
He reigned for forty-nine years
at the height of the Mongol Empire.

The surrounding garden is one hundred and fifty acres
enclosed by walls twenty feet high
pierced by four enormous gates.

The splendid gate of sandalwood seventy-four feet high
with four minarets of white marble
eighty-five feet high
at its four corners.

The mausoleum proper is a five storied building
surrounded by cloisters gleaming with white marble.
The roof is silver and gold.
A beautiful bronze lamp swings from the ceiling.
It is kept lit night and day.

Simply magnificent!

But why didn't his dynasty last?
Did he think his tomb would fix his place in history?

He planned his own tomb before he died.
Now he lies forgotten but for this splendour.

'The Son of Man has nowhere to lay His head.'
Yet all of history
divides
at the watershed
of His birth.

FRAGRANCE OF LIFE

Jemmie, laying out the frankincense
for the Mar Thoma Church Communion
was surprised
that I had never used incense.

At home, after she washes her thick, dark black hair
she makes a charcoal fire and adds incense
and encircling the coals with her wet hair
dries it so that her clean head
is fragrant with perfume.

At first I thought India was dirty.
More than that. I thought it was filthy.

But after some months I have learned
that India may be dusty.
But not dirty.

Indians are among the cleanest people in the world

>   whole families
>   stripped naked in Calcutta
>   soaped down and bathing
>   at the public water taps.

Some, like Jemmie,
carrying the unmistakable scent
of frankincense.

>   'Thanks be to God who leads us
>   wherever we are
>   on Christ's triumphant way
>   and makes our knowledge of Him
>   spread throughout the world
>   like a lovely perfume!'
>   II Corinthians 2: 14-16

Oh God, how can that be possible?

Are you able to so invade and pervade my life
that in my person
others
may discern the refreshing fragrance
and unmistakable scent
of Christ alive?

EARTHENWARE JARS

The homes in the village are spotlessly clean.
Most have large earthenware jars
much higher than my height
built into the kitchen.

Every day, twice a day, the women
fetch water from the well
and fill the large earthenware jars in their homes.

Or they may store some of the ground grain
in an earthenware jar
saving enough out for the evening meal.

The smaller vessels, used only at the well,
are aluminum, brass or copper.
You can judge the wealth of a family
by the quality of their vessels.

But in the end, who cares what the vessels are made of?
It's the contents that count.
Food.
And drink.

Help me to know myself
as an earthenware jar
O God
And not to confuse
my poor life — the vessel —
with your
Word of Life.

VEILS

I

t's a bit of a shock to see veiled women.
Why can't they be like me?

Even the girls here at the Ecumenical Centre
will draw the sari across their mouths and noses
in the presence of a dignitary.

A sign of modesty.

I suppose it might be rather interesting
to go through all of life
always peering *out* at other people.
But it's part of the culture I find hard to fathom.

UNWRA photo

26

And we without veils …
what do our faces reflect?

Anxiety?
Despair?
Frustration?
Boredom?
Preoccupation?

May my face
O God
reflect like a mirror
your presence in my life.

May my face
Christ Jesus
transparently announce to all
that You live in me.

May my face
Holy Spirit
be shining
with love and holiness.

They remove their shoes—
350 people sit crosslegged
on the carpet in the chapel.
Behind the Communion Table is a simple cross
and the picture of Jesus, the Liberator
brought from Canada by M.A. Thomas.

It is the Mar Thoma Syrian rite of 'Holy Qurbana.'
The body is a wafer
the blood is wine
dropped from a spoon directly into my mouth.

'Let us break bread together on our knees'
we sing, on our knees.

Embroidered on the table linen
is a lotus flower.

The lotus flower
opens when the sun is up
and closes
when there is no light and warmth.

I noticed that two Catholics
and even one Hindu
communicate.

The glow from the lamp
reinforces my feeling
of being at home
with other members of God's family
as we pass the peace
from one to another.

THE CUP

The visiting American girls were invited to an orthodox Hindu service and had difficulty getting the 'bindi' (the red mark on the forehead) to stick.
So one girl moistened her finger with saliva, dipped it in the paste, and found that it worked. Each in turn moistened her finger and scooped from the cup.

It was only afterward that the Hindus
were able to rescue the sacred vessel
and purify the cup
which had been desecrated
by unknowing foreigners.

It is so important that the *inside* of the cup be clean.

Isn't it the custom at Jewish weddings
to drink from the same wine glass
as a sign of the shared life
that awaits the bride and groom?

Oh Lord
you ask us
'Can you drink the cup I have to drink?'

Fearfully
and with trembling
we haltingly reply,
'Yes, we can.'

Berkeley Studio photo

The young man with only one leg
pauses hopefully beside my taxi.
I have been warned against encouraging beggars,
so I stare straight ahead.

Each day I write down my main impressions.

It is only in the middle of the night
that I suddenly recall that other beggar
whose neck is raw and red
who looks as if his head
was pulled too quickly from his body
at birth.

I guess I screened him out of my mind.
It was too horrifying a sight to think about.

But if I'm able to suppress memories of those two
it doesn't leave me free
because there are many more to take their place.

In the narrow streets of Old Delhi
suddenly
there's a man with his ear protruding from his neck.
Another, pushing through the passengers on the bus
has a hole in his neck
the size of my fist.

On the streets of Bangalore, young boys
whose legs were deliberately broken at birth

continued over

crouch on large 'skateboards'
and push themselves by hand along the streets
asking the nearest person for a penny
fated since birth for beggary, by someone else's decision.

The young deaf and dumb mute at the bus depot
hands out printed pamphlets
recording his family's hopeless situation.
Is he a fraud?
Part of a beggar's union?
Or is his story true?

In the West, we are protected from such sights
of abnormality and deformity.
No wonder I protect myself
by putting them out of my mind.
But in the middle of the night, they crowd in again ...

    'If you love those that love you, what good is that?'

Lord, you loved all those unlovely people
those marginal ones
the ones thrust beyond the bounds of normal society.

        But how can I possibly love them?
        What will it mean to love them?

I fear your judgement.
I fear the end-time when all those images
all those faces
will line up in procession before me.

        And in their faces
        in those 'images'
        I will see You.

P eople piled on people.

Church Herald photo

Five to a bicycle. Three to a scooter. Twenty to an ox cart. No hope of getting on a bus. Last man in hangs on to the extra man who is totally outside the bus! A bicycle with a carpet strapped on behind goes by.

People piled on people.

Squatting women weeding the Presidential gardens by hand. Women carrying loads of bricks on their heads, to restore ancient ruins for the tourist. Men playing cards at curbside. Men urinating on trees. Men pushing broken down buses.

People piled on people.

A young man with only one leg stops hopefully beside my taxi. A man whose neck has been so badly burned the head has been fused into the body. A nation of children turning into beggars in the cities.

People piled on people.

Wealthy women in beautiful saris attend the International Film Festival. Well-to-do men frequent large Western-style hotels. Knowledgeable people guide me through the Art Gallery. A Judge of the Supreme Court asks me to send him Canada's Human Rights legislation.

People piled on people.

Middle class girls trying to understand poverty. Students from Vellore Medical College entertaining us with the classical 'Bharatantyam' dance and modern 'rock' music. The fake snake charmer having his dancing bear handy when the tourist bus stops.

So many people—

Yet
'Even the hairs of your head are numbered.'

Lord I believe;
Help thou my unbelief!

ASSUMPTIONS

For breakfast, I have corn flakes and an egg.
The rest have 'iddali' (rice cakes) and 'sambar' (curry).

I was taught that knives and forks
are a mark of a civilized person.
But for eating, everyone but me
uses the fingers of the right hand.
Even Mr. Justice V.R. Krishna Iyer,
Judge of the Supreme Court of India!

And nothing is spilled, dropped or messed up.

I always assumed that a woman walking behind a man
meant subservience.
But I am told that in this part of India
it means that the man respects and protects her
by going ahead.
It's like a man in Canada walking at curbside
as a mark of courtesy.

Wherever did we get the notion that it was acceptable to
impose our norms on other people? How is it that we
think 'our' way is the right way?

Forgive us,
for 'thanking God that we are not as others are.'
Scatter our pride
and be merciful to us
sinners.

Often in the West, we express thanks
for our way of life
or we pray for those
'less fortunate than ourselves.'
But who are the fortunate?

The affluent, whose lives are spotted
with boredom and despair?
The comfortable,
who have lost the transcendence of life
and whose biggest problem is what to serve
at the bridge club tonight?

Or might the fortunate be found
among those poor wretched souls in Delhi
who, having survived yet another night of cold
wake, and thank God for the sun
and the day
and each other?

Are the fortunate our sons and daughters
who get drunk for kicks
and spend money to make themselves feel good
and drive recklessly
because they are glutted
with 'the good things of life?'

Or might the fortunate be a young Tamil girl
who has nothing
but gives me her bracelet
and buys me three small oranges?

How I wish all Your children
             had health
               knew joy
                   welled up with laughter
                       rejoiced in the grace of giving.

And knew what this short life is for.

               And God
      seeing all that was made, said
         'It is very good.'

BABYSITTING

The babies of India seem so small to me.

While standing in the heat, waiting for a bus that
eventually came two hours later, I noticed a small boy,
not more than three years old, carrying his little brother,
who was fast asleep, his head rolling on the bigger
boy's shoulder.

The older boy, the babysitter
had hands outstretched for pennies
by accident of birth
turned into a beggar
before the age of four.

When I admire the baby on her mother's shoulder
in the village
the mother smiles at me and says,
'take the child if you like him so much!'

It's not that children in India are unloved.
It's just that there are so *many* of them
so many mouths to feed.

How on earth can I help my own children understand
that their position
in relation to those Indian children
makes an absurdity out of history
and a mockery of justice!

The girls prepared skits to illustrate the questions they had about women's roles in India.

The first was about non-co-operation by husbands in disciplining children ... surely a trans-national problem!

The next, a husband wanted a male child desperately, though they already had four daughters.

There was the young woman whose further education could not be financed because the money was needed for her dowry!

And the young couple, living in the extended family arrangement, whose mother-in-law would not allow them to go to the movies.

Lois Wilson photo

These fine, middle class Indian girls feel trapped
                by dowry
                        by extended family
                        by parents
                        by history
                                by tradition.

Yet few of them know
how to become free persons.
In fact,
they are not so different from Canadian girls
who feel trapped   by family
                        by custom
                                by male expectations
                        by history
                                by their own self image.

Lord, You treated women as full persons.
You dignified the woman taken in adultery
and restored her pride.
You took Mary seriously
and discussed theology with her.
Yet you also appreciated Martha's care
for Your well being.

                How can I become a full person?
                How can I be free
        yet responsible to those I love?
                How can I know
                        what it means
                to be a woman?

PURGATORY

The slums of Calcutta are not as bad
as in Bangladesh
they said.

I talked to two old ladies:
They buy second-hand newspapers and cut them
into rectangular pieces
for re-sale to restaurants for take-out meals.

They work from six in the morning
till three-thirty in the afternoon every day
and the margin of profit
for two of them, per day
is three rupees.

As I left the older woman
squatting there on the ground
I knew her face reminded me
of someone I had seen before.

Three days later
I knew who it was.
It was the face of my father
just before he died.

The middle aged man, in ripped T-shirt and dhoti earns his living stringing garlands for Hindu shrines.

He gathers thirty neighbours' children
in his Calcutta slum home
for a backyard school
behind his one roomed hut.

The Observer/E.L. Homewood photo

Every morning, with the help of a large slate
the children are learning
to read and to write;
to protect themselves from diseases caused by poor water
to eat foods that will prevent malnutrition.

Then we visit six men meeting in a mechanics shop
after work.
They have banded together to dispense nutrition biscuits
to children on the street
who need this 'boost' in diet
for three months
to prevent deformities developing.

They bake the biscuits themselves
and volunteer their spare time.
They plan a bazaar to raise more money.

A young woman with a B.A. lives among the poor
in a one room hut
volunteering her time and expertise
to teach the illiterate.
She lives on next to nothing herself
and therefore is accepted.

When they ask me
'are there poor people in Canada?'
I'm suddenly struck dumb.

How can I explain?

Of course there are poor in Canada.
But they'll survive today and tomorrow.

                    In India
              the poor each day
              walk that thin line
                    between
                life and death
              hope and despair.

The Sri Lakshmi Narayan Hindu Temple in Delhi
gleams with white marble
and creates the sensation of a cool oasis
in contrast to the dust of the street.

Inside
a man dressed in western business suit
holding a child by the hand
prostrates himself before the image
of garlanded Lord Krishna.

I sit in the garden listening to the guru making music
and watch the brilliant sun
light up the red and yellow sandstone pillars.

And then there are the little temples
no bigger than our bathroom
or shrines set up outside
wherever 'peepal' and 'neem' trees grow together.

Here the cows are fed.
Here men sit and chat.
No wonder it's a shrine.
The shade of the trees refreshes body and soul.

One day there is constant music
wafting from a village three miles away.
It's part of the seven day marriage celebration for Hindus.

continued over

There is so much here I do not understand or appreciate.
Thousands of years of history and culture
communicated and sustained through epics
                                        music
                                        dance
                                    and custom
and a certain spirituality, possibly because
material things are so few.

It's so easy
and so arrogant
to think that God
speaks only English
and works only through Christians.

Help me, O God, to relate to those
of other living faiths
with openness and trust.

Let this be my first question:
            'How far has Your Spirit
            penetrated the life and witness
                of this person?'

Grant me the humility to listen
for *Your* answer.

Whenever you enter a village home in India
you remove your sandals
partly to save wear and tear on the mat
on which you sit cross-legged.

Before entering Hindu temples
you remove your sandals
as a mark of respect for the 'holy.'

Christian churches too, have adopted the practice.
To receive communion in the Mar Thoma service
we removed our sandals.

A guest at the Ecumenical Centre created
an international incident
when he decided *not* to remove his shoes
for chapel worship
thinking, thereby, to make a 'Christian witness'
against this Hindu custom!
All he did was shock
and hurt
the Indian Christians
who have adapted the cultural custom
of removing sandals
to indicate God's lively presence and grace
when they gather to worship.

'Put off the shoes from thy feet
for the place whereon thou standest
is holy ground.'

After experiencing the dry season
in South India
and having water in Madras only every second day
it was a relief to leave the dust behind
for the mountains
      lakes
         and snow of Kashmir!

We drove straight up the valley
           past rice paddy fields
          Lombardy poplars
           hay stacked high in trees
finally up the smoky trail
to the top of the mountain.

Gov't of India photo

Clear blue, cloudless sky, framed by white snow
and green lush pine trees.

I made snowballs.

Finally, at the very top
a Hindu Temple
sunk in eight feet of snow!
And peasants shovelling paths through the drifts
to allow would-be skiers a chance on the T-bar.

And then
the boat trip on Dal Lake
clear green water
bounded by magnificent snow capped mountains.

The surroundings restored my soul.

FREEDOM

I always thought I was a free person
free to be myself
                    to innovate
                        to push my horizons
                            until I saw beyond
                                the present limits of my life.

I always called myself a Christian
free to love others
to put the care of another before my own self interest.

But in Delhi, at the Qutb Minar
a fluted tower of red sandstone
built on the site of the first mosque in India
while I was admiring the intricate carving

a woman fingered my cape …
my cape from Wales …
the one I'm so proud of …
and she, a perfect stranger
and poor.

I pulled away, ever so slightly.
The other woman with her laughed …

                    'If anyone wants your coat
                        let them have it
                    and your overcoat as well.'

But there was no way I could give her my cape.
                    I was too cold.
                    I needed it.
                        It means too much to me.

The Observer/A.C. Forrest photo

Those are not the real reasons.

I was not free to give the matter a second thought.
There was no real decision to be made.
After all, it is *my* cape.

                  I am not free.

T he home is obviously a wealthy one.
We are greeted by
                            an adult retarded son.
                        One of the daughters is deaf.
                            Another crippled by disease.
An avalanche of disaster
has visited this Parsee family.
And now the father
                            in the prime of life
                            has died.

Traditionally, his body would be placed on a hillside
and stripped by the vultures.
But his widow believes this unrealistic
in an urban setting.

So she is breaking tradition.
She decides on cremation
despite the fact that Parsees revere fire
and see God in its dying and rising rhythm.

The Observer/Franz Maier photo

I offer a wreath of jasmine to the widow
who places it on the urn of ashes
and asks that I pray.
She knows I am a Christian.

Then the family pays last respects:

each placing a pinch of frankincense in the fire
each bowing deeply in prayer and supplication
each with palms together in a gesture
of final farewell.

The ashes are buried in simple ceremony
in a corner of the garden.
The grave is marked by drawing a circle in the dust
and garlanding with jasmine.

Later, I find out that this widow
out of her tragedy and despair
has given the land for a home
for the retarded
for the deaf
for the physically handicapped
for the aged.

I've always understood that You
Creator
can bring new life
out of death.

But this is the first time I've met a person
who put herself so much at Your disposal
to enable You to work Your miracles!

She is a Parsee.
So were the Wise Men.

I climb a mountain in Kashmir
with two companions
a Hindu youth and a Muslim woman.

The Hindu boy tells me how he can't get a job
because Kashmir is full of Muslims
who discriminate against him.
'Muslims are uncivilized!' he says.
'They cut off the noses of all our Hindu gods.'

My Muslim friend, on the other hand
tells me Islam
is much superior to Hinduism.
'We have to give alms to the poor,' she says.
And four other duties
though she could remember only three.

A Muslim boy is circumcised
and learns verses from the Quran.
A Hindu boy is taught Sanskrit
and has his head shaved.

Muslims eat the cow.
They consider the pig unclean.
Hindus eat pork.
They worship the cow.

Muslim women are often veiled.
Hindu women wear saris
and a red dot on the forehead.

History casts a long, dividing shadow between them.
And the shadow is religion
                    not race
                        or language.

Oh Lord,
forgive us those times in history and now
            when we use our religion
                to divide us from people
            rather than using our faith
                    to bring us all
                        together.

THAILAND

To
Gossip
the
Gospel

The Toronto agent is surprised that I have only carry-on luggage.

Toronto to San Francisco — five hours.

'We don't get a movie on this flight!' complains a teen in the waiting lounge. But he was wrong. We got 'The Hunter,' starring Steve McQueen, whose role was mostly to pursue the 'bad guys' and kill them. I didn't bother with the head sets. I got the message.

Milwaukee on the left
Chicago on the right.
Over Iowa, Nebraska, the Sierra Mountains.
Why can't Americans learn to *boil* the water to make tea?

San Francisco to Honolulu — five hours

I slept.
But I wake up to yet another movie, 'Urban Cowboy.'
Another drink offered. Another meal.
Finally, I hang a sign on me. 'Please do not feed.'

Honolulu to Hong Kong — eleven hours

Flight announcements in Chinese.
The first pink of dawn is tipping the wings of the plane.
My watch says it's 2:45 a.m.
That's almost twenty one hours we've been in flight.
Suddenly: spectacular Hong Kong Harbour!

highrises
clotheslines
inland canals
mountains

Hong Kong newspapers are full of measures to ban illegal
immigrants, including swimmers from the mainland.
750,000 squatters from China wait in the mountains.

Hong Kong to Bangkok — three hours
Twenty-four hours in the air!

According to the papers
Vietnamese troups are poised
on the Kampuchean border.

Finally. Finally I am here.
It's 12:30 p.m. in Toronto and January 4th.
It's 12:30 p.m. in Bangkok and January 5th.

How did that happen?

F rom a billboard
'Drink Canada Dry'
a red-coated Mountie urges me.

We take a fifty-cent bus ride from the airport to
the Central Mennonite offices.
It's hot.
Heat, sultry,
wraps me like the gas fumes from the bus.
Through the window,
a flitting peepshow
                    Women sweeping the streets
                        construction workers' shacks
women 'selling' birds to the faithful
who win merit by 'freeing' the birds.
Sidewalk merchants selling indescribable foods;
                        pineapple
                        papaya
                        tapoo
                            squirmy black ooze
            naked children at the roadside
            enormous elaborate temples
                flamboyant trees
                open air buses
                sarongs
                sandals
                    sweet orange tea
                        merchants hawking wares
                        palm trees
                            waterbuffalo
                                saffron-robed monks.

The women are so slight and delicate
yet some haul bricks on a construction site!

I'd forgotten how much of life is lived on the streets in Asia.
Here's a beauty parlour for women
There's a barbershop for men.

Middle class school girls in white blouses
                           navy skirts
                           black shoes
                           and white socks!

Loads of stores packed with consumer goods
for the rich.
The red-light district
where packaged sex-tours
welcome European businessmen.

And the traffic!
Tuk tuks
taxis
people darting across the street at risk of life and limb.

I visit a Buddhist temple.
To my left, a row of elderly ladies
with their heads shaved as clean as billiard balls.
And every one of them with a set of gold fillings!

                    We smile a lot
                and then withdraw.
      I wonder if we seem so strange to them
               as they to us?

GOSSIPING THE GOSPEL

Round brown leeches
    coconut
      fish
        chickens
          pork
            sweet fruit
              fried banana
                shrimps of all sizes
                crabs
                  grapes
                    octopus
                    swordfish
Pink Chinese pudding (it's nearing Chinese New Year)
Lettuce and carrots (for foreigners) potatoes, fruits
Brass; pottery; pewter - so cheap!

It reminds me a bit of the market
near my home in Hamilton
because it's such a sociable event.

It reminds me of the market on the way to Hoskote in India
set under enormous Banyan trees.
I buy and eat a red, sweet, prickly pear
and wander through the 'stalls'
with goods spread out neatly on the ground.
              Aluminum pots
                bangles
              jaggery balls
              betel leaves
Coal oil if you have your own container.
Old newspapers for re-sale and recycling.

continued over

Even New Testaments are sometimes sold
not for the Gospel, but for the *paper*!

Bus tickets are re-cycled in parts of India.
And we can't survive without Kleenex and toilet paper!

St. Paul found the market a good place
to 'argue daily with the passers by.'
He was accused of 'actually proclaiming Jesus
and the resurrection
in such a public place.'

Paul knew a few things ...
              markets are a great place to relax and talk
                this is where the currents of life are strong
                    people spend much time buying and selling
                        the 'good news' must be part of that scene.

Markets are a good place to gossip the Gospel.
So are laundromats.

                    Lord
        I'm so used to praying to You in church
                and talking about You
        to people who already believe in You
                    or say they do.
        How can I explain your warmth and love
                    to ordinary people
                    in the marketplace
                    in the laundromat
                        or office
                        or factory
                        or hospital.
        Wherever there are people for whom you died.
                Help me to know how!

KOREA

**Signs
of
the
Times**

GETTING IT BACKWARDS

Why don't you go to Bangkok
on your way to Korea?
It's in the same general area, isn't it?

Well — vaguely!

I go from thirty-four Celsius in Bangkok to below freezing
in South Korea. Culture shock hits me the minute I settle
into my hotel room. The drinking glass in the bathroom
is 'disinfected' for the guests.

That strikes me as slightly obscene in contrast to what
I saw in the refugee camps and the Thai villages
yesterday. And here's a shoe polisher. Just what I need
for my sandals.

The Korean tourism book has this to say:
'Christianity looms large in the foreground in Korea
through its identification with
                    modern education
                        international technology
                        and western values.'

Does Christian faith really condemn us
'to make good?'
Isn't that getting it backwards?

We're *not* to glory in our
                    wisdom (modern education)
                        might (international technology)
                        riches (western values)

but to glory in our 'knowledge' —
our covenant with the Lord
who is loving kindness
      judgement
           righteousness   Jeremiah 9: 23-24

Lois Wilson photo

We remember before you
those in South Korean prisons
beaten with branches till they can't stand
prevented from sleeping for 38 days
'encouraged' to make fabricated confessions.

The journalists and broadcasters
denied the right to broadcast news.

And yet, 'Christianity looms large' in this country?

Deliver us from believing
in whatever kind of god suits us.
Nurture us in risking
for the God
of our Lord Jesus Christ.

When Joseph was sold into slavery
by his brothers
                no one trusted anyone anymore
                family relationships broke down
                phones were tapped
                students spied on professors
                no one could speak openly.

When Jesus was falsely accused
                the innocent suffered
                judges gave judgement for a bribe
                sons were arrested for working with the poor
                lawyers jailed for defending prisoners.

When Jesus was mocked
spat upon
hit on the head with a reed
and crucified
                many were horrified, but silent
                some were beaten, never to work again
                some suffered mental and emotional derangement
                some had their fingernails torn out
                at 'purification' places
                where 're-education' took place
                some 'disappeared' forever off the face of the earth.

                The torturers gave up their humanity.
                The land was filled with tears and anguish.

'My son was taken for "spreading false rumours." It cost
200,000 Won to reclaim his body.
Every bone was broken.'

continued

'I was beaten so badly, I can never work again.
Many others are paralyzed or deranged mentally.'

'My lawyer husband defended prisoners.
As a result, he himself is now in prison.'

'We hosted Human Rights meetings in our building.
So we have endured five-month jail sentences.'

'My son signed a petition requesting clemency
for the condemned. He too was arrested.'

brutal violence
fingernails torn out
suicides
false confessions

It is the ultimate betrayal
of Korean against Korean
of brother against brother
of sister against sister.

Why?

To keep the situation stable?
To protect the economic freedom of the multinationals?
To attract foreign investment?
To make sure the 'economic miracle' of South Korea
will flourish?

It really means the freedom of the poor
to starve
the freedom of the outspoken
to be tortured.

THE ABSENCE OF GOD

The father told me he was nineteen.
'His grave faces beautiful snow-capped mountains.
The night we heard the shooting downtown,
I urged my son not to go. Not tonight.
But he said, "this is the night I must go.
This could be the liberation of South Korea."
The soldiers had surrounded the city for a week.
One of them in a field near my house told me
he'd had only rice for three days.
But plenty of rice wine.
And the orders were; "If every soldier kills five citizens
then the problem of Kwangju will be solved."
They shot my son with an M 16 rifle
but he didn't die immediately.
So they beat him till his eyes popped out.

Didn't Jesus say, "One life is worth more
than the whole world?"
They piled the bodies in trucks
both the living and the dead.
Common graves.
Many never had a service of committal.
But we had a service for my son.'

Incredible courage!
Incredible faith!

The taxi driver who drove us to the cemetery would not
accept a fare. It turns out he knew this bereaved father.
The taxi driver's son only received a light sentence.
Not execution!

continued over

Koreans
killing
Koreans

'I wouldn't have believed it
if I hadn't seen it with my own eyes.'

Muddy road to the cemetery
past the infamous Kwangju prison
Where both my companions had spent 'time'.
No heat in those prison cells
but the cheerful bell from the Buddhist Temple
greeted each new day.
Little girls waving cheerfully
as we passed the rice fields.
The traditional curved roofs of the houses
are beautiful.
Men are at work digging a grave nearby
carting the clay away in huge wicker baskets
on their backs.

The father asked me to say a prayer at the graveside.
                But I was spiritually paralysed
                        by a sharp sense
                    of the absence of God
                        and I pleaded
                'Will you pray for *me*?'

Gleaming, shimmering tinsel
Christmas trees in the hotel
graceful flowing dresses
wonderful food
enormous modern hotels
flea markets
super-highways
snow-capped mountains and big wide rivers
cold — cold — cold
sweet green eggs
mandarin oranges
squid
Ginseng tea
and *mad* traffic!

But there are also the memories of horror
lips pierced with a ball point pen
when there's a refusal to answer interrogation
hung by the arms
naked
beaten unconscious upside down
attempted suicide by beating head on the cement floor
and ears still bleeding when visited in prison
letters not received.

Will I ever return to Korea?
Must I return?

What is the meaning
of undeserved suffering?
Is it the birth pangs
of a new creation?

77

Many countries today are lovely
for the unseeing tourist
who looks at life through the glass
of a tour bus
or from the balcony of a 'luxury hotel'
arranged through a reputable travel agent
                    predictability and comfort
                    hot baths
                        and souvenirs for friends.

Many countries are sheer horror for the seeing visitor
who brings a different vision to our times
who works with the poor
committed to a new heaven and a new earth
who faces unpredictability and suffering
                no water
                    and betrayal of friends.

'Why can't you interpret the signs of the times?'

Matthew 16:4

The rest, who play it safe, never speak openly.
That's most of them.

South Korea is a lovely country
especially for the tourist who looks at life
through the glass
of an air-conditioned bus.

            Whether you are able
            'to read the signs'
            depends on the vision you bring.

CENTRAL AMERICA

Alternatives to Revolution

I can't stand the thought
of four hours at Miami Airport.
So I hop a public bus for Miami Beach.

Miles of sand
           surf
               shells
                   hibiscus
                       oleander
                           palm trees
white people trying to turn brown
brown people waiting on them
miles of hotels — all built on sand!
Later I find out it's a carbon copy of Rio
Hawaii
the Platinum Coast of Barbados.

As we take off
the view above Miami is spectacular
                     causeways
                         hotel high-rises
                             turquoise sea
                               coral reefs
                                   bottle-green sea
                                     tufts of islands

At last — land — miles of superb beaches
and ridges of inland mountains
small towns in the valleys
and snake-like brown rivers.

Down through the clouds to Tegucigalpa, in Honduras.

In the line-up through customs
eight youthful Mormons in three piece suits and ties
with four zippered Bibles and books of Mormon in Spanish
are whisked away by a senior Mormon.

The signs at the airport tell me
            use 'Visa'
                drink 'Pepsi Cola'
                    'Rotary International meets Thursdays'

Military planes and helicopters
practise manouevers
and a grade 'B' movie blinks
on a television set.

It's all so strange
except for the
                three-piece suits
                Visa and Pepsi Cola
                Rotary International
                the TV movie

        How can we sing the Lord's song
            in such a familiar land?

Several stops on the road to Bilwaskarma
to remove a huge snake
to wait for cows to cross
to have the car searched for guns
(we don't have any)
unbelievable ruts
mud and 'bridges'
a flat tire
we visit briefly with two women who administer
a nutrition centre for ten mothers and children.

The farther north-east we go
more grass
less dust
beautiful pine trees
cool breezes and lagoons

Our partner church here is the Moravian Church
and I greet two Miskito Indian congregations
on behalf of the United Church of Canada.

We join the youth under the trees
singing to guitar music
and watch the Sunday School
act out the Old Testament story
of 'spying out the promised land.'

A pot-luck supper introduces me
to the church leaders in literacy
                              Christian education
                              youth work
                                   a regional organization.

Some have been trained theologically
in the Bible College.
They also receive training
in typing, carpentry and practical skills.

Treated royally to a meal of
cassava, boiled banana, chicken, rice and fish;
(the head is the main delicacy). I pass!

I leave for the trip south to Puerto Cabezas
         proud of the contribution our church is making
                    and honored to work
                    with our sisters and brothers
                    of the Moravian communion.

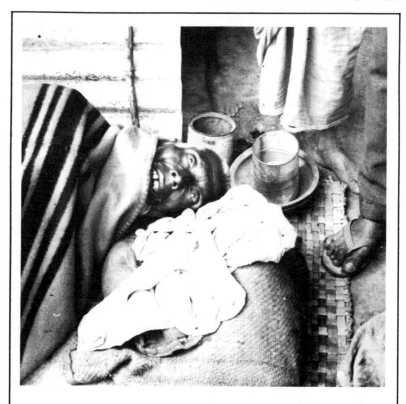

I have seen it before.
     I have smelt it before.
     The smell of hopelessness
of indescribable poverty.

I don't take a picture.
I already have a picture
     of garbage
      open sewage
      snotty kids
      loafers

but where did I take it?
Jamaica?
Rio?

Shacks of corrugated cardboard
old planks thrown together for a roof
hordes of Nicaraguan youngsters
questioning me with their eyes.

'Be careful where you step.'

The one distinguishing mark of this barrio
is a memorial stone at the street intersection.

'To a martyr of the revolution
age nineteen
died July 16, 1979'

The hopeful signs?
a mother
a seamstress who has lived in the barrio
for fourteen years
has a loan from the churches
and from her sale of dresses
supports fourteen people.

A man, a mechanic
has a loan from the churches
and by repairing motorcycles
supports nine people.

People shaping their own future.
Signs of hope!

W hat shall I say to him?
To my thirteen year old son
who wants to join the militia?'
This man's family survived the Nicaraguan revolution.
His wife and children fled to Costa Rica for two months.

For an entire day
the whole family
hid under the bed in their suburban home
while planes strafed the area
and Somoza's tanks invaded the next street.

Three youthful freedom fighters sought sanctuary.
They *all* would have been shot
if they had been discovered.

There were Sherman tanks in their suburban street.
So the family simply walked out
leaving everything
not knowing the future.

Through it all,
the father worked with the churches
to distribute food to over two hundred and fifty
bombed-out people.

And his young son, secretly
in the garage
fashioned Molotov cocktails to destroy those tanks.
Without telling his parents, of course.

But now he wants to join the militia.
What shall Christian parents answer?

The United Church Observer photo

ARGENTINA
PERU
CHILE

The
Electric
Toothbrush

IMAGES OF BUENOS AIRES

L a Boca, home of the 'tango'
statues of the Virgin Mary *everywhere;*
enormous soccer stadiums;
pale blue jacaranda trees in bloom;
ombu trees with branches sticking straight out;
ten lanes of traffic one-way in the middle of the city;

> More theatres than in New York
> pizzarias by the platterful
> Japanese gardens
> planetarium
> ballet
> art
> sculpture
> matté tea
> royal palms

Rio de la Plata is a river too wide to see the other side!
Fishermen at the river and an empanada shop.

The face of old Europe in the facades of old houses.
Bouganvillea in Britannia Park.

> This beautiful city would be so much nicer
> if I didn't know that at this very moment
> people are being
> tortured
> here.

CHRIST LIVES

A five-minute radio program every day
to Buenos Aires.
But it's censored.

Tapes of the program go to prisons
and hospitals.
In the past year, two programs have been taken off the air.
One on unemployment and bankruptcy
the other a Christmas program: The Magnificat —

'And Mary said
My soul doth magnify the Lord
      And my spirit hath rejoiced in God my Savior.
            For he hath regarded the low estate
                  of his handmaiden
                  for behold, from henceforth
            all generations shall call me blessed.
      He hath showed strength with his arm
            he hath scattered the proud
            in the imagination of their hearts.
      He hath put down the mighty from their seats
            and exalted them of low degree.
      He hath filled the hungry with good things
            and the rich he hath sent empty away.'

That's too explosive
to be broadcast in Argentina today!
If too many people knew
that God wants *that* for the world
they might join God
                  and turn the world
                  upside down!

I'VE BEEN HERE

A country too poor to fix its buildings
and it can't afford to tear them down.

The horror of the shacks
                of mud and bamboo
                        of cardboard and sticks
                            of tin and mud
and every sort of garbage holding down the roofs
because there are no nails.

Again, I decide *not* to take a picture.
I've seen it all before.
Was it in India?
Or in Trinidad?

We fly to Inca Country
fourteen thousand feet above the sea
The ruins of the fortress of Sacsahuaman remain
a hint of the dignity of the Inca Empire
before the Spanish conquest.

In the Plaza D'Armas is a huge 15th century Roman
Catholic church, with a solid silver altar.
                Immense wealth
        a pulpit carved from cedar by an artist from Europe
                a picture of the Lord's Supper,
                with a guinea pig in place of bread
        St. Peter in an incredibly ornate purple robe.

I can't help contrasting this with the immense poverty of
the remaining Inca Indians.
                one tugging a llama
                        another making yarn from a spindle

or posing for a picture
all for the benefit of tourists
and for their charity.

Why on earth did the Spaniards drag enormous mirrors
and pipe organs from Europe, across the Atlantic,
through Panama and over the Andes to this valley?
And at what human cost to the peasants?

With such a history
is it any wonder South American Christians
now speak of God
who frees the oppressed
and loves the poor.
Not in the next life.
But now.

Who
'exalts them of low degree
and fills the hungry
with good things'.   Luke 1: 52

I wonder if they realize the horror
of what they are telling me?
Or is it so commonplace now
that never a ripple is stirred?

It's what's happening to the
children
of people in prison.
It's what's happening to the
children
of 'disappeared' persons.

Sometimes the children have been given away to someone
before the grandparents are aware of it.

It's still going on
the imprisonment and torture
a man age 65 detained 45 days
hit with a rubber truncheon by drunken soldiers
he and others
forced to shout out the Lord's Prayer
even though some were Jews.

Three were handcuffed.
One became so thin in prison
he eventually slipped out of handcuffs.

One girl had studied with a Jew, so was accused of
subversion and imprisoned. A child of ten cares for five
younger ones since the parents 'disappeared.' A
grandmother, 76, cares for four children under
seven years of age.

And what to tell the children about their parents?
Other kids ask,
'Where is your father? your mother?'

In schools, children are asked to write essays
celebrating the army
and the service of the military to the people.
Can you imagine the rage when,
after twenty years
the children discover what has been done to them?

'Suffer the little children
to come unto me
for of such
is the Kingdom of God.'

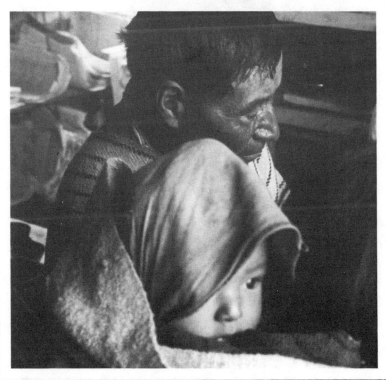

UNICEF photo

A TALE OF TWO CITIES

Santiago — 'It is the best of times ... '

I recognize the ads.
I might as well be back in Kingston, Ontario
            Orange Crush
                Singer Sewing Machines
                    electric shavers
                        electric dryers
                            TV's and stereos
                                electric blenders
                                    Jello 'that sets in 15 minutes'
                                    floor polishers
                                        baby shampoo
Goods that even with forty months to pay,
most people in Chile can't afford.
There are a few in this wealthy city, the owners of all that
TV advertises, who consume half of all the goods and
services of the country.

The poor
            live in barrios behind discreet fences
        or beg on the pedestrian shopping malls
                or work for a dollar a day
to refurbish the face of the city.

And refurbish it they have
                    with statues
                    fountains
                        freshly painted buildings
                            elegant skyscrapers
and shopping arcades with the latest electronic gadgets
from all over the world!

continued over

'It is the worst of times. . .'

They line up at soup kitchens
Or beg for a few centavos
in exchange for a tune on the accordion
or embarrass bus passengers
by stretching out their hands
after a rendition of a popular song
or hawk caramels and fruits on the streets.

Two cities in one:
                    the electric toothbrush
                    and the soup kitchen.
            That is *not* what God intends.

EATING TOGETHER

I gave up asking what I was eating.
'Sea creatures' they would say.
Or 'You don't have this food in your country'.
Usually it was good!

    rice
      beans
        empanala
          frijoles
            tortillas
              pedemoleque
              jack fruit
            papaya
                watermelon
               casava
                 boiled banana

Just once
when I innocently removed the cover from a dish
was I shocked.

'It's a delicacy
the head of the fish is the best part'
said the Bishop
very gently.

I have one but it doesn't work.'
That, said Bob McClure, should be the second verse
of the National Anthem of developing countries.

> Washing machines
> saw mills
> German-made busses
> telephones
> roto-tillers
> toilets
> none of them work.

Crossworld photo

No spare parts or mechanics are available.
'It can't be helped'
a friend apologizes
to me, a western technological woman
      who expects
        showers to work
          toilets to flush
            airlines to run on time
and whose closest experience of the frustration of third
world citizens to inappropriate technology was the
breakdown of the summer cottage's old refrigerator
thirty miles from town and
no spare parts manufactured anymore.

        What are we supposed to do, Lord?
        Keep our technology to ourselves?
        Negotiate its use with our partners?
             Or what?
        And why is it so difficult
          to 'do good?'

BRAZIL

**The
River
of
January**

THE RIVER OF JANUARY

Is there any other city like it?
The magnificent harbour rivals that of Hong Kong.
They say all the boats of the world can get into it
at one time.

Wall-to-wall skyscrapers
favelas tumbling down the mountain side
juts of rock
gorgeous rugged coast-lines
miles and miles of beach
roads snaking through mountains

It's 34 Celsius. A Madonna statue on every mountain top
crime (hang on to your purse!)
subway and commuter trains
ice-water in the fridge at the Methodist Seminary.

At the Methodist Church in the favella Rochinha
there is garbage lying
waiting for the rainy season
to wash it down the mountain side.
The church has 63 pre-schoolers in day care.

Eighty per-cent of the people migrated from the northeast
after they were forced off the land by agri-business.

Opposite the church is a pool-hall. 200,000 people live
in the favela. A few streets away is the Intercontinental
Hotel and apartments with four bedrooms each.
We drive past the fenced-in Sheraton pool; past
Copacabana beach; past the slum facing the ocean where
the Pope visited (after electricity and water had been
installed).

From Corcovado, the statue of Christ the Redeemer,
and a quarter-page ad in the Jornal do Brasil which says
'Come unto us
all ye who deserve a Chevrolet'.

Rio suffers from all the modern conveniences
pollution
traffic jams
crime
too many people.

The early explorers thought the harbour was a river
so they called it the River of January (Rio de Janeiro).
Justice does not roll down
the River of January.

A COCKTAIL PARTY

Three local Protestant ministers were invited but they couldn't come tonight.'

'I would like to introduce myself, because I am one of the few in this room who goes to church once in a while.'

'Do you know such-and-such a minister in Canada? He buried my father.'

'Are you acquainted with the Church of England?'

'Is The United Church of Canada like The Church of Scotland? I used to attend it in my younger days.'

'Are you here on business? Oh *that* kind of business! I'm surprised your church works with Roman Catholics. It certainly wasn't that way in Canada when I lived there, twenty five years ago.

'No thanks. I'll stick to wine so I can function. I just came from a delightful Japanese party. *Everybody* was there.'

Suddenly I am right back in the superficiality of middle-class Canada.
Small talk.
Or church talk.
But not person talk.

Mercifully, I find two people to talk with.
The newly appointed president
of a Canadian company in Brazil
will talk disarmament and labour relations.
One woman confesses she is overcome with
                    the poverty
                        the robbery
                            the violence
                                the murders
but that she can't blame the poor,
since they are literally starving
and sometimes must rob to eat.

It's the shock of coming so directly from talking with the
poor (who go to church), and then talking with some of
the 15,000 English-speaking business executives (who
don't go to church anymore).

I thought
when I received the invitation
that I might be able to talk about some issues.
But it turns out to be a cocktail party.

'I wanted you to hear the other side,' my host tells me.
'But that's what I hear in Canada,' I protest.
'The reason I came to Brazil is to hear the "other side"
                    from the peasants
                        the shanty-dwellers
                            and the women.'

Thoroughly depressed, I am chauffered back home.
On arrival at my room
                    I weep
                    and pray
        'Make me faithful to the Lord of history!'

Three rooms. Seven people.
The mother proudly shows me four baptismal
and three profession of faith certificates.

They left the drought-stricken north
and journeyed to the city
        where it would be better
          the polio stricken child might walk
       the one retarded because of meningitis
         could manage better
and perhaps the teenage girl could finish grade three.

But it was a tough journey.
Father died two weeks after arrival.

Then they met someone
        who offered them three rooms
    who arranged a bricklaying job for the young man
         who brought joy
    to the eyes of the boy with meningitis.

Then they planted a few flowers in the churchyard
        underneath the clothesline.

Aramco photo

They say in Rio
that if Jesus had visited
he would never have told the parable
of the houses built on sand and on rock.

Jim Taylor photo

Because in Rio, the situation is reversed.

The tourist hotels are built along sandy beaches
the tumbledown favelas of the poor
are built on the rocky waterless mountain tops.

It's obscene!
This tourists' paradise
is but one short block from
       stench
          heat
             overcrowding
            garbage
               indescribable poverty
                people locked in.

No exit.

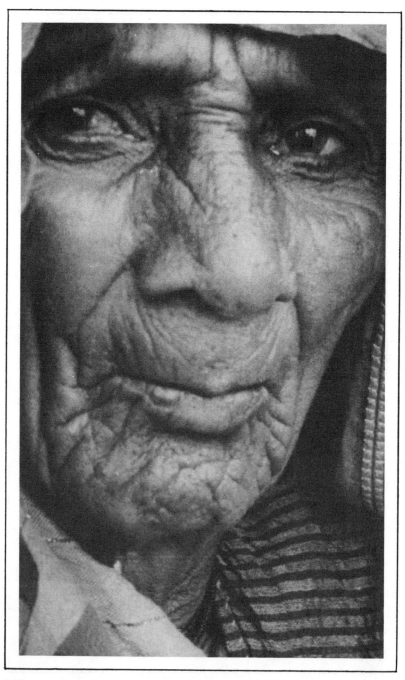

A FAVELA IN SAO PAULO

The shacks are perched on stilts
over the harbour.
They are built on garbage from the city.
                    Stench
                    Heat

A carpenter fashioning a table for the 'school'.
A fourteen-year-old teaching a five-year-old how to read.

                    Stench
                    Heat

Most women have fifteen children.
Only five live.
Is my memory slipping
or is this place indeed *worse* than India?
It's certainly worse than the refugee camps in Thailand.

                    Stench
                    Heat

Naked babies playing in the mud.
At least they're cool!

'Would you find money for a school for us?' a man asked.
I have to say 'no'.
There are thousands of places that need schools.

            But I am glad to get out
            of the stench and the heat
            and from under his pleading eyes.

C arnival!
soccer stadiums with partisan crowds
                    gaiety
                        humour
                            music.
Pine trees with arms reaching heavenward, and high
green terraced hills; watermelons; lots and lots of
Virgin Mary statues.
Enormous Catholic churches, contrasted with the small
1874 Protestant Waldesian Church.

Favellas
surrounding day-care centres in Methodist Churches.
Gauchos.
Washing strewn on bushes to dry.

United Church of Canada photo

Helpless poverty in the polluted shanties
Hopeless poverty among the peasant farmers.
Half the population
receiving less than one-tenth
of the total income.

Wall-to-wall high rises
super highways
industry
pollution in Sao Paulo.

Hot strong sweet coffee
heat
savage exploitation and a booming economy.

But in the midst of it all
50,000 'base communities'
of the Roman Catholic church—
people meeting regularly in homes
around the 'Word.'

Prayer and politics
the salt of the earth.

FLINTSTONES IN RIO

The 'Flintstones' pranced
to a dubbed Portuguese sound track.
A Stone Age family but they have
                    a car
                        a washer
                            a refrigerator
                                a stereo
                                    a TV
all cut out of stone!

Earlier, I had watched a procession of TV ads for
                    electric shavers
                        stereos
                            floor polishers
                                electric blenders
                                    electric hair dryers
all the benefits of western civilization
offered to those who live in the slums of Rio.

In Canada
mired in a consumer society
insulated in a thousand ways from the poverty of our poor
I am only mildly insulted by such a program.

But in Rio, exposed to
                    garbage
                        hunger
                            hopelessness
                                immense suffering
            I think the 'humour' is obscene
            and the export of our 'way of life'
                    demonic!

In Cuba, I needed a Spanish translator.
In India, one who could speak Malyalam.
In Nicaragua, a Spanish translator
and one who could speak the Miskito Indian language.

At a meeting of the Moravian Church in Nicaragua,
the eight people present required five translators!
I missed a lot through translation.

In South Korea, a Korean translator.
In Brazil, the World Day of Prayer was in Portuguese.
In Chile, it was in Spanish.

The world is a tower of Babel.

At my first meeting of the World Council of Churches
I noted that many spoke in their own tongue
but understood each other!
Sometimes without a translator.

Does that mean that the international Christian community
is the normal expression
of Christ's body?
And the national churches
are the abnormalities?

Pentecost is God's intention.
Not Babel.

GOING HOME

It
Only
Takes
A
Spark

ONLY A SPARK

Twenty young people in Brazil
squashed into a small room
singing to guitars.

'Inflation is our biggest problem,' they say. (It's 144%).
'The church is for the old.
The young prefer sex and drugs.'

But some want to know,
'How can we help the poor?'
'What do you mean by the 'end time'?'

We try all sorts of songs
to see if we can hit on one I know.
Finally

   'It only takes a spark
    to get a fire going
   and soon all those around
   can warm up to it's glowing.
  That's how it is with God's love … '

Jim Taylor photo

118

We sing in Portuguese and English
We pray in Portuguese and English
We eat Brazilian 'sweets'.
We laugh and find a universal language.
We know ourselves to be part of the body of Christ.

Seventeen young people
in eight canoes on Lake of the Woods, in Canada.

'Sex and drugs are our biggest questions.'
'The church caters to the old
and doesn't encourage youth.'
But some want to know
'Who was Jesus, really?'
'What does God want for my life?'

We sit around a campfire
long after midnight
and watch the sparks
leap up into the sky.
We sing and pray
and eat peanut butter sandwiches.
We laugh together, and find a universal language.
We know ourselves to be part of the body of Christ.

Touch our lives
with tongues of fire
and send your Spirit
to heal your hurting world
so all shall sing
pray
laugh
and know each other
as sisters and brothers
in Christ.

I had been warned
Security Police would be monitoring my sermons.
(They told me this *after* I had preached.)

At the airport the next day
all bags were searched.
The only thing they took of mine
was a small ragged piece of paper
my sermon notes from the night before!

The text was from the Psalms
and spoke of the pilgrimage
to 'Jerusalem'
in search of community
through justice.

After several futile efforts to have my notes deciphered
they returned them to me with the comment

'It's only about Jerusalem anyway!'

A red pump
gushing fresh clean water.
We ford a stream
and see the woman
washing clothes the way they did in Bible days
the way most women still wash clothes
by beating them on rocks.

continued over

The United Church Observer photo

In South America
            I didn't drink water for five weeks.
            Five weeks without fresh water!
Instead
            Orange Crush
            Inca-Cola
                sweet, strong coffee
                mineral water
                        pineapple or papaya juice
but no fresh water.
My own choice, mind you.

                When I got back to Canada
                        the first thing I did
was drink fresh water.

In India
where the wells are deep, some villages have two wells.
One for Harijans (formerly the untouchables)
and the other for the rest of the village.

During the hot drought in Madras
I had water only every second day.
When I washed my right hand before eating
I poured just a little water on it.
Water is too precious
to be squandered by using a wash basin.
Having a bath is another story!

In Nicaragua
I flushed a toilet by pouring water into the bowl by hand.
Do you know how much water it takes
to flush it *once*?

So many people's lives are lived at a survival level.
It's like wilderness camping
but *without* sparkling lakes
or rolling rivers.

We miss the meaning of Jesus' talk
of 'living water'
of His gift becoming a 'spring' inside us
'welling up into eternal life.'

We assume water comes from a tap
hot and cold
running
always.

Lord,
with all our wealth
we still search the sky
for the promise of showers.
We long to be washed
in your living waters
so that
'justice shall roll on like a river
and righteousness
like an ever flowing stream.'

AFTERWORD

How "fortunate" we are in Canada!
I have trouble with that cliche.
I have trouble with the word "fortunate."

How "affluent" we are in Canada--yes.
How "isolated" we are in Canada--yes.

But "fortunate?"
That smacks of the Pharisee who "thanked God I am not as other men are."

Or do we imagine our wealth and freedom of expression makes us and our society superior to others?

When we do finally recognize the beam that is in our own eye Then there are a few tentative steps we can take:

- Pray more intelligently for the needs of people in other parts of the world, now that we are aware of their real situation.
- Use "For All God's People" - the Ecumenical Prayer Cycle published by the World Council of Churches for congregational use, as a useful aid, Sunday by Sunday.*
- Expand your personal friendships. In almost every Canadian community there are persons of "The Third World"— India; Chile; Caribbean; native Indian; disabled; etc. Get to know them and learn from them. Intentionally break out of your accustomed circle of friends.
- Evaluate your life style — your eating habits; the kinds of gifts you give; the quality of time spent with your family. Many people in the world fast once a week, for physical as well as spiritual reasons. Try it.
- Develop some "mutuality in mission" initiatives in your congregation. Invite the non celebrities, the marginalized,

* Available through The Book Room, United Church House
85 St. Clair Ave. East, Toronto
or Anglican Book Centre, 600 Jarvis St., Toronto.

the "out-of-touch" to share insights with you. Work together with people of other living faiths (Islamic, Hindu etc.) to determine what needs to happen in your area to create authentic community.

- Be aware of human rights legislation in your province, and know how to support persons from minority groups when needed.
- Commit yourself politically, and talk with your MP, not just about more aid, but the necessity of structural changes in Canada's trade policies. Do some serious reading on this subject.
- Commit yourself theologically, and contract with some others to read and struggle with the meaning of faith as you read the Bible together. There are lots of aids: David Lockhead's "Living Between Memory & Hope", and K.H. Ting's "How to Read the Bible" for starters.
- Commit yourself to understanding the world through the eyes of others, as well as through the eyes of those of us who are "fortunate!" Here is a beginning list of periodicals to subscribe to:

The New Internationalist --a World Development magazine
113 Atlantic Ave., Brooklyn, NY, 11201 1yr: $19.00

Inter-Church Committee on Human Rights in Latin America
40 St. Clair Ave. East, Toronto, Ontario

Fish Eye Lens - Ecumenical Forum
11 Madison Ave., Toronto, Ontario

One World - World Council of Churches
150 Rue de Ferney, Geneva, Switzerland

And perhaps you will move from
"how 'fortunate' we are"
to
"God, be merciful to me, a sinner "
to
a redeemed life.

Also from

Wood Lake Press

AN EVERYDAY GOD

by **James Taylor**

Deeply moving and sensitive...
clear, Biblical, personal
meditations by one of Canada's
most articulate Christian writers.

$5.95

A GUIDE FOR USE BY LEADERS
OF ADULT STUDY GROUPS
BY K. GRANT KERR $2.50

"For me, **An Everyday God** is all the things a book of this kind should be and rarely is. I look forward to reading it each day, and must actively resist the temptation to read it through in one sitting. Dorothy picked up several copies to leave with friends. My daughter says, 'It's not corney—it's really good'."

**Garth Mundle, Principal,
St. Stephen's College,
Edmonton.**

Wood Lake Press
S-6, C-9, R.R. 1
Winfield, BC
V0H 2C0
Canada